Batik

6

206

2010

Batik

Sarah Tucker

The Art of Crafts

First published in 1999 by
The Crowood Press Ltd
Ramsbury, Marlborough
Wiltshire SN8 2HR

British Library Cataloguing-in-Publication Data

A catalogue record for this book is available from the British Library.

ISBN 1 86126 2639

The illustrations on pages 9 and 10 are reproduced with the permission of the Oriental and India Office Collections of the British Library

Typeface used: Melior

Photography by Philip Chambers, Colin Tucker
Designed and typeset by Focus Publishing, Sevenoaks, Kent
Printed and bound by Leo Paper Products, China

Contents

Preface

WHAT IS BATIK?

Batik is a resist method of dyeing and decorating fabric. Hot liquid wax is painted on to fabric to prevent the dyes from penetrating the fibres. If the fabric is white to start with, any lines or shapes painted on the fabric in wax will preserve the colour white. After dyeing with a pale colour, more wax is painted on to some of this coloured area to preserve it before the next dyeing.

Batik is therefore a process of repetition by which a design is gradually built up through successive dyes, starting with the lightest and ending with the darkest colours.

The distinctive marbled effect so characteristic of batik results from the wax cracking so that the dyes penetrate the cracks. This can be controlled by both choice of wax and by careful handling of the waxed cloth.

My Personal Involvement with Batik

I came to batik by a chance meeting with a friend who had discovered a wonderful batik tutor, Sonia King. I was persuaded to come to a class and was instantly hooked. I had been working in the theatre as a company manager but had paused to have children, and I thought batik would be a minor diversion before I returned to proper work in the theatre. That was twenty-five years ago, and I never did return. Instead, batik changed my life: I became addicted to it, and I remain obsessed, fascinated by the endless possibilities offered by dye and wax.

What this Book is Setting Out to Achieve

I hope this book will inspire others to become, as I am, addicted to the batik process. I enjoy the exciting challenge of balancing technique with design, and I hope to infect you with it, too. Once the basic techniques are learned, you will find that the batik process adapts to produce a very personal style. Moreover, as a method of decorating and patterning cloth, the possibilities for experimentation are endless. For instance, the finished batiks may end up as garments, cushion covers, lampshades, wall hangings or as pictures, stretched or dry mounted.

This book explains the various basic techniques of batik in such a way that a beginner can gain confidence in the process. There are seven easy to follow step-by-step projects, some offering the more advanced student a greater understanding of the potential of batik.

Opposite: Overlapping hands design

1 A Brief History of Batik

The precise origins and age of the batik technique are not possible to date accurately. Textiles, by their nature, are fragile. The oldest fragments of batik that have so far been excavated were found in Egypt; they were indigo-dyed, and date from the fifth or sixth centuries A.D. Old batik specimens have also been discovered in Japan, and it may be that batiks were being produced in China in the sixth century A.D. and exported to Japan, Central Asia, the Middle East and India via the Silk Route.

The origins of batik may be disputed but it is the Indonesians, especially in Java, who are known to have taken the techniques to imaginative lengths to produce a unique art form. 'Batik' as a written word dates back to sources from the early seventeenth century, occurring for the first time in Dutch records. The word 'batik' is thought to come from the Javanese word 'ambatik', derived from 'tik', which means to mark with a drop or spot. It was also the Javanese who developed the canting – originally spelt 'tjanting' – as a tool: unique to Java, and again probably dating back to the early seventeenth century, this tool gave an astonishing precision to the detailed motifs. Although the Javanese style was influenced and enriched by the decorations and symbolism of many cultures, the canting offered the possibility of dense patterning, of painstakingly drawing in wax thousands of dots and fine lines.

Traditionally, batik was used to decorate fabrics worn as garments, as a sarong folded or draped around the head, shoulders and waist. These fabrics often have significant symbolic value expressed by the colours and ornamentation used in their design; patterns may have ceremonial or religious functions, or indicate the power or status of the owner. Many batik designs were therefore not intended for everyday use, but were reserved for important functions, weddings and ceremonies. A number of motifs were reserved exclusively for the court. The symbolic meanings of the designs were often as important as the ornamental value. Less intricate batiks were worn by both men and women as everyday dress.

Traditionally, men prepared the fabric and women did the waxing, sitting on low stools with the cloth across their

An illustration from Raffles The History of Java, showing a dancing girl wearing batik.

Right: An illustration from Raffles *The History of Java*, showing a Javanese warrior wearing batik.

knees supported in front by a cross-bar frame. Cracking or marbling, which we think of as batik's distinctive look, was regarded as a sign of poor workmanship. The wax was removed by boiling after each dyeing and reworked and re-dyed for every colour; this method meant that the wax did not build up in layers, and resulted in minimal cracking.

After the colonization of Java by the Dutch in the early seventeenth century, batik production spread to Europe via Holland. The first serious study of the batik industry in Java was made by Sir Thomas Stamford Raffles, who became the British Governor of Java for a brief period in the early nineteenth century when the Dutch possessions were placed under British control during the Napoleonic wars in Europe. He was very interested in Javanese culture, and in his book *History Of Java* he included significant information about batik patterns and designs.

Fashion buyers back in Europe were enthusiastic about this exotic look, and by the 1830s several factories had been established in Europe to produce imitation batik. Practitioners from Central Java were imported to Holland to teach workers in the textile industry the batik technique. Using engraved copper plates and rollers, cheap imitations could be produced which even showed the fine cracking.

Competition from the cheaper European imitations was countered in Java by the invention of the tjap, or cap, in the mid-nineteenth century. This is a block set with a raised copper pattern, and whereas formerly the batiker had worked for three months on a length of fabric using a tjanting, the cap printer could finish in one day. Repeat designs could be waxed at speed. As a result a batik industry arose in Java around 1850 which could compete in price with the European imitations.

The next significant change occurred in the 1920s when synthetic dyes started to replace traditional vegetable dyes. These helped to make the dyeing process faster.

Economic problems during World War I hit the batik market in Europe; even in Indonesia the effects of the economic crisis were clearly felt, with one workshop after another closing down. After the war, re-establishment began with the Batik Research Centre in Yogyakarta, and Java now has many small and several large factories producing for the tourist trade. Small workshops give Javanese artists scope for fine innovative work, since they are no longer restricted to traditional designs.

The possibilities of batik as a medium for fine art are being exploited by contemporary artists all over the world. The techniques have been freed from the traditional formal styles, offering total freedom of design and expression. Schools in Britain offer batik as part of GCSE art courses, and many adult education courses in batik are on offer across the country. The Batik Guild, formed in October 1986, currently has over 170 members, made up from both professional and amateur artists, all with a keen interest in wax and dye.

2 Essential Theory

In batik one works from light to dark. Many of my students find this difficult to grasp, but it is absolutely essential. This means that when designing a batik, you have to plan in reverse – in other words, the areas you actually paint with wax are those on which you do not want the next colour to appear. This book will include simple step-by-step instructions in order to help students grasp this essential requirement.

Batik is not an exact art, and one of its chief attractions is the spontaneity of the process: you have to adapt as you go along. It is therefore a mistake to have too preconceived an idea of how the finished work will look. You will find many guidelines in this book, but batik is meant to be fun: experiment, see what happens, see if it works.

Understanding Colour

For me, colour is the most exciting aspect of batik, and the reason why I am so addicted to the process. When teaching, it is such a pleasure to watch students as they first introduce colour to their waxed fabric. Working from light to dark, each colour is going on top of another, constantly changing and transmuting the design. You will discover how one colour works in

Dyed fabrics showing the three primary colours, the three secondary colours, and brown.

relationship to another, how one colour can change the appearance of another, and how colours affect texture and depth. Illusions of warmth, cold, happiness, anger or calm can be created by the expressive use of colour. A basic understanding of colour theory is helpful, and it is absolutely essential to know how colours will combine with others.

The primary colours are red, yellow and blue, and these three colours cannot be obtained by mixing other colours.

The secondary colours are orange, green and yellow, and these can be obtained by mixing two primary colours. For example, blue and yellow produce green, the complimentary of red. The three primary colours together give brown.

By trial and error, variations of all colours are possible. (*See* the later chapter on mixing dyes for batik.)

Health and Safety

It is essential to observe good health and safety practices when working with hot wax and dyes.

• As a general rule, good ventilation is essential.

• More significantly, the paraffin wax used in batik is highly inflammable when molten, and care must be taken not to let it overheat. Keep an eye on the thermostat on the wax pot, and turn it down if any smoke appears. Also, there is a risk of acrolein fumes being released if the wax is overheated, and these can cause severe respiratory problems.

• If you are accidentally burnt by splashes of hot wax, hold the burn under cold running water for five minutes. Do not peel off the wax immediately, as it acts as a barrier to bacteria.

• Good ventilation is particularly essential when ironing out the wax. Preferably do this work near an extractor fan.

Above: Dyed fabrics.

• When using textile dyes it is important to wear rubber gloves and an apron.

• Dyes can cause asthmatic or allergic reactions in some sensitive people, and generally you should avoid any risk of getting them in or near your mouth. Wear an appropriate respirator or dust mask if you are susceptible.

• Open dye lids carefully, and always add the powder to the liquid, and not the other way round.

• Cover the work surfaces with newspaper: these can be thrown away if dye powder is spilt.

• Do not consume or prepare food or drinks in the areas where dyes and chemicals are prepared or used.

• Immediately wash off any dyes that come into contact with the skin.

Dye and chemical suppliers are required by law to issue safety sheets with all their products. These should be requested when buying for the first time, should be read carefully, and kept in an easily accessible place in case you need to refer to them quickly. If in doubt, contact the manufacturer for advice.

Opposite: Poppy picture with coloured fabrics in the foreground.

3 Basic Equipment

Fabric

Any natural fibre is suitable for batik; most artists use cotton or silk. I personally prefer to work on cotton lawn, because it is a fine fabric and wax penetrates the fibres easily. Batik can be tried on many thicker fabrics provided they are not man-made, but you must realize before you begin that it will be more difficult to get the wax to really penetrate the fibres of calico or linen. Dyes react very well with cotton, and an added advantage is that cotton can be subjected to boiling, which gives added flexibility to the work. In the step-by-step projects later in this book I suggest that you use a fine cotton lawn except for the cushion cover project (project 5) where I propose using cotton velvet.

Wax

Beeswax or paraffin wax can be used, or a mixture of the two. Ready-mixed batik wax is available from craft suppliers in beaded form. Wax can be melted and re-melted over and over again.

Wax Pot or Heater

A thermostatically controlled wax pot is ideal, and can be bought from specialist suppliers. You can, however, use an electric frying pan that has a built-in temperature control. It is essential that the wax is only heated to the right temperature and does not approach

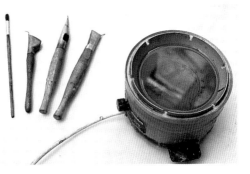

Opposite: Basic batik equipment.

Left: Thermostatically controlled wax pot with a selection of cantings and a bristle brush.

Left: Thermostatically controlled electric frying pan.

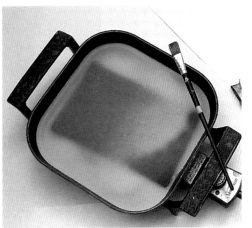

Far left: Three pots of wax: clockwise from the top, a prepared mixture of beeswax and paraffin wax; paraffin wax; and beeswax.

Cantings:

These tools are invaluable for drawing lines and making dots with molten wax. Their name used to be spelt 'tjantings', but they are now more commonly called cantings. They originated in Java, and they come in a variety of shapes and sizes.

boiling point, and if you use a wax pot the thermostat keeps the wax at a safe temperature. A cheap alternative is to use a tin of wax placed inside a saucepan of boiling water over an electric ring, though I cannot honestly recommend this method: it is clumsy and potentially dangerous, there is no temperature control, and the water has to be topped up regularly.

Frames

The fabric needs to be stretched and held taut on a wooden frame with drawing pins. An adjustable batik frame is ideal and can be bought from specialist suppliers, but it is easy to make your own non-adjustable frame by simply nailing and glueing lengths of wood 2cm by 4cm (0.8 by 1.6in) to make a frame of the size you require. A small range of sizes of home-made frames will allow you to work on two or more projects at once, and will increase your versatility.

A selection of cantings.

Brushes

You will need a selection of bristle and natural hair brushes for applying the wax. Other watercolour and sponge brushes should be kept separately for painting on the dyes – they should never be accidentally put in the wax pot.

An assortment of bristle brushes for waxing.

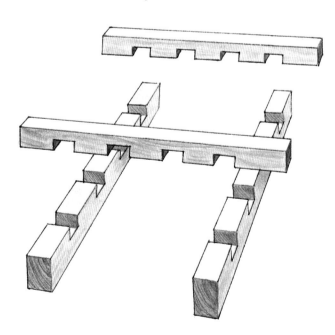

A wooden frame for stretching the cloth.

A selection of foam and paintbrushes for dyeing.

Dyes

• Cold water fibre-reactive Procion dyes are ideal for batik. They are permanent, easy to use, and are particularly suited for use on natural fibres.

• Direct and acid dyes are often used to dye cellulose fabrics, but as they require hot conditions to fix into fibres they are not suitable for batik because the heat involved would melt the wax.

• Naphthol dyes can be used for batik, although they are unsuitable for protein fibres such as silk and wool. These dyes are applied in two stages, first by dipping the fabric in a base solution and then in a diazo salt solution; the colour develops in the second bath. Vivid dye shades can be achieved but the process is complicated; if you want to try out these dyes I suggest you go on a specific course.

• Natural dyes can be used in batik. They are obtained from various plant, animal or mineral sources, and require a mordaunt to fix them to the cloth fibres. Perhaps one of the best known plant fibre dyes is indigo. (*See* later chapter for further details).

As I personally use mostly Procion fibre-reactive dyes in my batik work, I am concentrating on their use in the step-by-step processes in this book. Choose the three primary colours brilliant red, brilliant blue and brilliant yellow, and add navy blue, turquoise and mahogany. (*For more information* refer to the chapter on using the dyes.)

Spoons

For measuring dyes, and for stirring. If you are using spoons from the kitchen, remember to make sure they are properly washed before going back into the kitchen drawer.

Chemicals

For fixing dyes. The three chemicals I use are urea, soda ash and sodium bicarbonate. These need to be stored in screw-top jars, and labelled clearly and carefully using a waterproof pen.

Above: Chemicals for fixing the dyes: clockwise from the top left, soda ash in a screw-top jar; sodium bicarbonate; and urea.

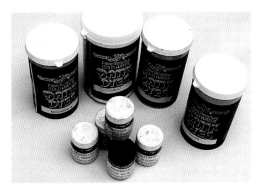

Above: Procion fibre-reactive dyes in containers.

Newspaper

This is essential for protecting the work surface and the floor. Batik is inevitably a messy process.

Kitchen Roll

Useful for catching wax drips and for blotting excess dye.

Rubber Gloves

Essential protection when working with dyes. Procion dyes will colour your hands, and purple fingers may not always be appropriate. It is also advisable to wear an overall or dark-coloured, old clothes.

Empty Yoghurt Pots or Jam Jars

These are useful receptacles in which to mix dyes and to wash brushes, and it is a good idea to have a range of them in differing sizes. Palettes are also useful for mixing colours.

Plastic Buckets and Containers

Use buckets and old washing-up bowls for dip-dyeing. Old baby baths are a good shape for dyeing larger pieces of fabric.

Plastic Clothes Line and Plastic Pegs

Alternatively you could use a plastic-coated airer, with newspaper underneath.

Pencil

I find that a soft lead 2B pencil is ideal. You should, however, avoid drawing a lot of detail with a heavy black line as the lines may remain under the wax.

Hair Dryer

This appliance is most useful for speeding up the drying process, though it must be used on a low temperature to avoid melting the wax.

Scissors

For cutting fabric.

Masking Tape

For keeping frames clean and can also be useful in designing shapes.

Iron

You will need an old non-steam iron for ironing out the wax from the fabric, with newspaper or newsprint to absorb the wax. Do not use your best steam iron unless you positively want wax in your clothes.

Notebook

For recording recipes and ideas and for quick sketches.

4 The Batik Process

HEATING THE WAX

Wax for batik can be beeswax or paraffin wax or a mixture of the two. Beeswax is very soft and pliable – it bends with the fabric and does not peel off – but it does not produce any cracking effect. Paraffin wax, on the other hand, used on its own, is very brittle and cracks easily. It is therefore a good idea to experiment with different combinations to see the different effects created by varying the proportions of the two kinds of wax: the more cracking required, the greater the proportion of paraffin necessary in the mixture. I personally favour a mixture of ¾ paraffin wax to ¼ beeswax. Ready-made special batik wax is available from craft suppliers in granulated or bead form.

Wax has to be melted before it can be applied, and it needs to be kept at a constant temperature of between 120 and 130°C; great care must be taken not to let it overheat. The correct temperature is essential so that the wax remains safe and yet penetrates the fabric satisfactorily. I really recommend buying a special thermostatically controlled wax pot or using an electric frying pan that has a built-in temperature control. I have been lucky enough to pick up a couple of these very cheaply at car boot sales and find them most useful. Although it is possible to heat the wax in a tin inside a saucepan of boiling water over an electric ring, great care needs to be taken not to let the water boil dry. It is important to keep the level of water up to the level of wax inside the tin in order to maintain the correct wax temperature.

Whatever method is used to melt the wax, if it is not hot enough it will not penetrate the fabric of the material, it will just sit on the surface and will not form a resist. This can be judged visually: when correctly applied the wax looks translucent, but if it looks opaque or whitish it has not gone on hot enough and has not penetrated the fabric.

Never leave a wax pot unattended. If the wax becomes too hot it can start smoking, releasing toxic fumes into the atmosphere. Be very careful.

USING THE TOOLS

The basic tools used in batik are cantings and brushes.

Cantings

Cantings – or tjantings – are special Javanese tools for applying the wax; they behave rather like pens. The melted wax is held in a small copper bowl and fed down either a single, or several capillary spouts; the handles are made of either wood or bamboo. These tools are ideal for drawing lines and for making dots.

Cantings can be bought with a variety of sizes of spout. If the hole in the end of the spout is wide, I find that too much wax flows and it is difficult to control, so when choosing a canting look for one with a small hole so that you can achieve controlled fine lines. My own

TIP:

Crackle can be controlled by using more, or less beeswax in the composition of the mixture of waxes. Use more paraffin wax for more crackle. Add more beeswax to make the wax more pliable and less prone to cracking.

preference is for a small tool called a kystka used by the Ukrainians for decorating eggs with wax; it is very like a small canting, and I find them invaluable for fine work.

It is essential when using a canting to have a piece of tissue in your hand when you carry the filled tool from the wax pot over to your work, so as to catch the drips and to stop them going in the wrong places. Carefully wipe the excess wax off the base of the canting to avoid drops accidentally falling on your design.

Using a canting with a tissue in the other hand in order to stop drops of wax falling onto the fabric.

To get the feel of the tool, practise first on some newspaper. Keep the canting moving steadily once it has made contact with the fabric – the waxed line should look translucent. If the wax looks white and opaque, it is too cool and is only lying on the surface. Turn your workpiece over to check the back to see if the wax has penetrated completely; if it has not, scratch off the opaque wax and re-work with really hot wax. Return the tool to the wax pot frequently and hold it there for a few seconds to heat up again. Inevitably there will be a few blobs of wax that fall in the wrong place. In most cases the best solution is to try to incorporate the mistakes into

something positive; otherwise you can attempt to rub them away with your fingernail, although you will find that wax is very tenacious once it is in the fabric. If it is essential that blobs be removed, you can usually scratch out most of the wax, then pour a little boiling water through the material just where the mistake lies. This works well while the material is still white; however, once it has been dyed the colour is liable to run, unless enough time has passed for the fixing process to be complete.

The spouts of cantings do sometimes become blocked. I find fuse wire, or the wire that is found running through the centre of the ties used to close polythene bags, perfect for unblocking. Poke the wire through the spout while it is hot.

Brushes

Where cantings are useful for drawing lines and making dots, brushes are needed for filling in large areas of wax. The spontaneity of the brushstroke is also very good for creating a sense of movement. Once they have been used for waxing, brushes are pretty useless for anything else, so choose your brushes with care. The best brushes to use for batik are made of bristle. Some softer hair or synthetic brushes do not hold the wax satisfactorily, but are ideal for painting on dyes later. I find that for wax, the stiffer the brush, the better.

Again it is necessary to keep returning the brushes to the wax pot, in fact even more so than with cantings – essentially for every stroke. Do not pause for thought with the brush in the air because it will lose heat very fast, and if then you try to work the wax, it will be too cool to penetrate the fabric. However, do not leave brushes in the wax pot for a long time as they will burn and begin to lose their bristles.

Various other effects can be created

TIP:

Fill the bowl of the canting only about half full so that the wax does not spill over the top when you are working.

Opposite: paper collage pictures and scarf.

by using unusual brushes, even household ones. For example, try using a toothbrush or a washing-up brush – though be careful to shake off excess wax onto newspaper first. Other textural effects can be achieved by using unconventional but simple home-made tools: try cutting a strip of latex foam and tying it round a stick; or cutting into rolled-up paper towels and using them to transfer hot wax onto your fabric. Again, shake off the excess wax first or your tool will be overloaded and the wax marks you make will be blurred. Screwed-up and crumpled paper can also be effective for making marks, and likewise cotton buds. Try several of these and decide which you like best.

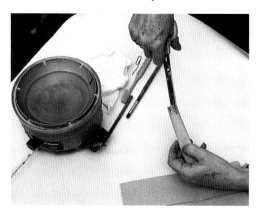

Cutting a paper towel to make a hand-made tool for applying the hot wax.

Using a paper-towel tool.

To create a different effect, you can etch lines in the waxed fabric with a pointed metal tool, though be careful not to make a hole; for this reason avoid tools with too sharp an end – an opened-up paper clip works very well and is less likely to damage the fabric. You may have to etch on both sides of the fabric to allow dye to find a way through the wax.

Etching into wax with an opened-up paper clip.

Many Indonesian batiks consist of repeat patterns made by stamping with a block or cap.

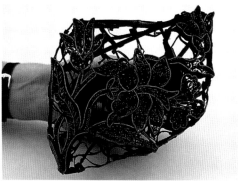

An Indonesian cap.

These blocks are set up with a raised intricate copper pattern used to print the wax resist on the front and back of fabrics. You can experiment with making your own blocks: any object which conducts heat and which has a clearly defined shape can be used. Try banging nails or zig-zag metal joining strips into wood or cork to create your own repeat patterns. You may also be able to find old typesetter's blocks, which are ideal for batik.

The fabric needs to be stretched and held taut on a frame before you can work with it; an adjustable batik frame is ideal. Pin the material onto the frame using drawing pins or special silk pins – these have three prongs to minimize the risk of tearing your fabric – in such a way as to keep it flat and smooth.

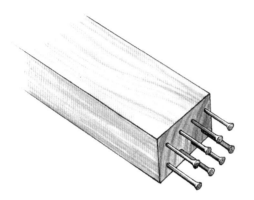

A home-made tool: nails in a block of wood.

Stretching the fabric onto the frame using drawing pins to hold it in place.

Selecting and Preparing Fabric

Fibres can be classified into two groups: natural and man-made. The reactive dyes used in batik only react with natural fibres, so it is essential to check that your material is all natural. A burn test is a good way of identifying fibres: a natural fibre will burn and produce soft ash, whereas synthetics melt into black beads. Natural fibres are divided into plant fibres, which are composed of cellulose, and animal fibres which are composed of protein. Cellulose fibres include hemp, linen, calico, cotton and viscose rayon; protein fibres are silk and wool.

When you buy fabric it is often treated with a dressing which needs to be washed out with hot, soapy water before any dyes are used. Although you can use and experiment with any of these natural fibres, I recommend a fine cotton lawn as a good material to start with.

Working with Silk

Many batik artists choose to work on pure silk; it has a beautiful texture and sheen and is particularly graceful when worked as a hanging or to make scarves. Silk painters will be familiar with the gutta resist process, in which a gum-like substance is drawn onto the silk with a nozzle to form a line of resist. The advantage of using wax, and therefore batik techniques, is that you gain flexibility in design because you are not restricted to single lines – with wax you can work in large and bold shapes. Silk is a very beautiful fabric, but it is expensive, and another disadvantage as regards the batik process is that it cannot be boiled; this limits its flexibility as compared with, for instance, cotton. Procion dyes also have a tendency to be muted when used on silk, as the fibres do not absorb as much dye as cotton fibres. For those wishing to work on silk I would recommend using dyes which have been prepared specifically for use with silk; they may need to be fixed by steaming or with an iron. These dyes are available from specialist shops.

Dyes and Dyeing

I use cold water fibre-reactive dyes; these take their name from the fact that they chemically react with the molecules in the fibre to form a permanent bond. 'Fixation' is the name we give to the synthesis which takes place as the fibres react with the dyes, the chemicals, the water and the oxygen in the air; this takes place over twelve hours as the fabric dries. A warm, humid atmosphere is best for the accomplishing of this process. Note that if the fabric is rinsed before completion of the fixing time, the dyes may not be fast and may run out.

When properly fixed these dyes are fast to light and to hand-washing, and can actually be boiled. They were first marketed in 1956 by ICI under the name Procion. The fixing of Procion dye is important, and most batik artists have their own preferred recipe. Mine is as follows:

- 1 tsp urea
- 1 tsp sodium bicarbonate
- ½ tsp soda ash
- Dissolve in a little hot water, then add to 1½ litres of cold water.

This liquid is your fixative. Urea is a dye dissolver, and enables the dye to spread rapidly and evenly through the fabric; it comes in granular form. Soda ash is an alkali, and is the catalyst which is necessary for the chemical reaction to take place; it is a concentrated powdery form of common washing soda crystals. Both soda ash and urea can be bought at specialist craft shops.

Once mixed with the dyes, the fix has a life of only three to four hours, after which time the chemical reaction will not take place; if used after this time there is a big risk that the dyes will wash out. Obviously the best policy is to make up very small quantities of dye; then it will not be wasted. Separate soda solutions and urea solutions may be kept in large quantities if the air is kept out, but personally I do not keep chemicals mixed in this way.

An alternative method of working is to keep the soda ash as a separate solution in an airtight container – it keeps for weeks with no apparent reduction in quality – and to apply the soda first and then the dye. It is primarily the addition of soda as an alkali that begins the chemical reaction. Many batik artists pre-soda their fabric. A soda fix is made up as follows: 1 heaped tablespoon of soda ash is dissolved in 1 pint of boiling water and then added to 5 pints of cold water. The fabric can either be soaked in the soda fix and wrung out, or stretched on a frame and painted with soda fix before the first dye is applied. Always rinse and re-soda after the third coat of dye.

The advantage of this method is that, since the dye solutions contain no soda, they do not deteriorate and so there is less wastage.

DYEING TECHNIQUES

There are many techniques to dyeing, and most will be explored in the stage-by-stage projects. Essentially, however, you can paint directly onto cloth, or you can dip-dye; and you can paint on wet or dry cloth, or you can mix dye with a thickener. To make up a dye, proceed as follows:

Take a yoghurt pot half-full of fix and add a quantity of dye powder: the amount you add varies, depending on the strength of colour required. Remember you should work from light to dark, therefore the first dyeing will be of pale colours whether you are dip-dyeing or colour washing or direct painting. A few grains of dye in half a cupful of fix will be enough for the first colour, or quantities in this ratio for a larger piece of fabric. Gradually add more and more dye until the final dark dye may well require two full teaspoons of dye powder to a similar quantity of fix.

Dip-dyeing: Traditionally, batiks were dip-dyed for every colour change. The process is slow, and restricted by the need to work in a careful sequence of related colours. The advantage lies in the subtlety of colour tones that can be achieved, and the marbling effect characteristic of batik.

In dip-dyeing it is not necessary to mix up a deep dye bath – just make sure that all areas have been in contact with the dye. The dyes react so speedily that the fabric can be lifted out of its dye bath within minutes; however, the reaction process continues during drying and for this reason the drying period should not be hurried. Hang the fabric from the edges on a washing line and allow it to dry naturally away from direct heat and out of the sun. If the fabric falls in folds there will be streaking. Do not place the cloth on a radiator, as the dye will react with the metal causing unsightly dark stripes.

Hand-painting dyes: Dyes should be painted on with the fabric still stretched on its frame. The advantages of hand-painting the dyes rather than dip-dyeing lie in the variety of different colours that can be introduced onto the fabric in one session of dyeing.

The step-by-step projects that follow will explore all aspects of these two different methods of dyeing. Whichever method is used, always wipe excess dye droplets from the waxed material to prevent them seeping under the wax layers. Finally, after the last dye has dried and fixed and been left overnight, rinse thoroughly under running cold water to remove the excess dye which the fabric cannot absorb.

HEALTH AND SAFETY

It is important to remember the health and safety aspects of dyeing. Reactive dyes in powder form can sometimes cause allergic respiratory reactions, therefore always keep the lids firmly closed on the dye pots, and always add the dye to the water, and not the other way round. You may want to wear a dust mask. Once mixed with water Procion dyes are not hazardous, but even so, remember to wear rubber gloves and old clothes. Protect the dyeing area with newspaper or polythene. Finally do not eat or drink in the workspace, or allow anyone else to do so.

DYE COLOURS

Fibre-reactive dyes come in a variety of colours, and although essentially you need only the three primary colours, namely brilliant yellow, brilliant red and brilliant blue, I would advise buying just a few more to give variety. I would add a navy blue to give depth of colour, and turquoise and mahogany to give subtlety. My students laugh at me for loving mahogany so much, but it can be used as a subtle rose pink when pale, it can be added to blue and yellow to make an olive green, and it is very useful for final full strength warm red-brown shades.

Using a Thickener

On some occasions when painting on dye you might like to experiment by using a thickener: this is used to control dye flow so that colour can be painted onto a precise area without bleeding. Dyes will normally spread even if painted onto dry material, and they may also dry to form a hard edge. Wax lines prevent spread, but you may find that in a particular design, a wax line is not desirable between areas of colour. The most commonly used thickener is known by the trade name Manutex RS; it is an alginate gum powder obtained from seaweed.

- ½ litre cold water
- 1 tsp Calgon (water softener)
- 2 tsp Manutex RS powder

Dissolve the Calgon in a little warm water and add it to the ½ litre of cold water. Slowly add 2 teaspoons of Manutex, stirring continuously for five minutes until the gum has an even consistency. Leave to thicken for 1 to 2 hours before using.

When ready to use, take a few teaspoons of gum and mix with a little fixative (urea, soda ash and sodium bicarbonate; *see above*). Now add your dye powder, the quantity depending on the shade required: you are now ready to paint the thickened dye onto your fabric. Leave in a warm place to dry for twenty-four hours before washing out the thickener in warm water.

Dyeing with Indigo

Used for creating shades of blue, indigo is one of the oldest vat dyes; originally it was obtained from various plants, however now it is available in both natural and synthetic forms. It is not for hand-painting.

Indigo will dye all natural fabrics and is therefore ideal for batik, although it is not a very easy process to set up. A large dustbin-type container with a lid must be made up as an indigo vat, and this needs to be checked to keep the indigo in good condition. Indigo is affected by the cold, and it needs a correct balance of alkalinity – it is also very smelly! Oxygen has to be excluded from the vat by means of a thick layer of polythene under the lid.

The process of dyeing with indigo involves wetting the fabric and carefully lowering it into the vat with tongs, being careful not to make air bubbles. The strength of colour attained is dictated by the length of time the fabric remains in the vat. Wet, the fabric will appear greenish-yellow, but as soon as it comes into contact with the air the dye will start to oxidize, and simultaneously the fabric will turn blue. Hang it out to dry to allow the oxidizing process to be fully complete. Brush the surface bloom from the fabric. Re-dip to darken, or dry and wax and re-dip.

To make an indigo vat you will need:
- Dustbin with lid
- 300g salt
- 20g caustic soda
- 90g indigo grains
- 60g sodium hydrosulphite
- rubber gloves
- wooden tongs
- washing line and pegs

MIXING THE INDIGO VAT:
Dissolve 300g salt in the vat with 2 gallons of boiling water. Add 3 gallons of cold water. Dissolve 20g caustic soda in cold water, stir and add to vat. Sprinkle 60g of sodium hydrosulphite onto the surface and gently stir in. Add 90g indigo grains. Cover the vat and leave for two hours.

Take special care not to introduce any air into the vat during the mixing process.

Discharge Dyeing or Bleaching

It is possible to remove colour from a previously dyed fabric by using household bleach. Some reactive dyes are extremely resistant to being bleached, particularly brilliant yellow and turquoise; nevertheless as a process, bleaching offers another possibility of changing the colour of unwaxed fabric.

It is often very difficult to achieve a really good final black dye using Procion dyes; black tends to be the least stable of all the dyes and has a tendency to fade to grey or green. An experiment involving waxing ready-bought black cotton lawn or black cotton velvet and then bleaching it back to off-white avoids this problem, because where the wax is, the fabric remains black. (*See* the step-by-step project.)

Household bleach can be used on cotton, but take care that the chlorine does not destroy the fibres. Dilute the bleach with cold water at half and half consistency, and paint or sponge the solution over your fabric. Watch for a reaction – do not leave for more than five minutes. Rinse thoroughly and then rinse again in a neutralizing solution of vinegar. Rinse finally to remove all traces of the vinegar.

Caution: Wear strong rubber gloves, and do not inhale the chlorine fumes. If any bleach comes into contact with your skin, wash immediately in plenty of running water. You may wish to wear safety goggles to protect your eyes from the risk of splashing bleach. Wash the rubber gloves after using bleach. Do not use bleach on silk as it will totally disintegrate.

Recording and Sampling

A sample book can enable you to learn from previous experience. In it you should keep all samples and scraps of design, in each case noting the dyes used, and how particular effects were achieved.

MAKING A COLOUR CHART

A basic colour chart is invaluable when learning about colour. I suggest the following method:

- Stretch a sample piece of white cotton over a frame.
- Use empty yoghurt pots as containers to mix three strengths of each primary colour: pale, medium and dark. You will need nine pots, three for each colour.
- Fill each half-full of fixative.
- Add 1 tsp of dye powder to one to make the strongest colour. Stir with a teaspoon.
- Add ½ tsp of dye powder to the next to make the medium dye.
- Add ¼ tsp of dye powder to the next to make the palest dye.

Do this for each of the three colours: you will now have three yellows, three reds and three blues in different strengths.

Your colour chart is achieved by first waxing an outline of a big rectangle.

Making a colour chart.

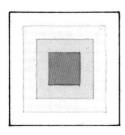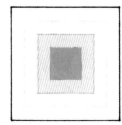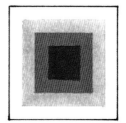

Paint in the palest colour to completely fill the rectangle.

When dry, paint wax in a band round the outside edge of the pale colour. Then paint medium strength dye into the middle.

Dry, then wax again to keep this tone, leaving a space in the centre for the darkest shade of dye.

Iron when dry, and leave to fix for twenty-four hours; then boil to remove all the wax.

Any colour must be dry before it can be judged properly because the dyes dry lighter than they appear when wet. The effect of applying wax brings back the depth of colour of the wet fabric. If, finally, you are going to be removing all the wax, the loss of tone needs to be compensated for and each dye made a little bit stronger as you go along.

Removal of Wax

Once you have applied the last dark dye and almost the whole fabric is covered in wax, it is necessary to remove the wax to see the design clearly. This is an exciting time, as it is really only now that you can see how successful the whole process has been. Before removing the wax, however, it is a good idea to rinse the batik in cold running water to remove excess dye not absorbed by the fibres. Dry the batik and then use a hot iron to remove the wax. I use a cheap non-steam iron especially for this, as you do not want to get wax on your best iron.

You will need a lot of newspaper and some clean newsprint or lining paper to cover your ironing board. Good ventilation is essential, so take care to work near an extractor fan or an open window. Lay several sheets of newspaper over the ironing board, and then make a sandwich of your batik between sheets of clean newsprint or lining paper. Then simply iron the wax out of the batik so that it is absorbed by the paper. You will have to keep replacing the waxy sheets from above and below the batik until wax no longer comes out.

Depending on what you decide to do with your batik, you can either leave it with this small residue of wax in it, or you can then boil or dry-clean it. If you intend to frame or stretch the batik it is quite feasible to leave a small quantity of wax in the fabric, because wax gives a richness and depth to the colours. If, however, you have made batik for clothing or for soft furnishing, then of course you need to remove all the wax. Provided the dyes have been fixed properly, the batik can be boiled.

BOILING THE BATIK

You will need a large old saucepan, soda crystals and washing-up liquid. Heat the water to boiling point in a large pan, then add a tablespoon of soda crystals and a good squirt of washing-up liquid. Using tongs, lower your batik into the boiling water. You may have already ironed out most of the wax from the material, but it is not essential to do this – it can be still covered in wax. Bring the water back to the boil, agitate the fabric for a few seconds and then remove it with the tongs. Rinse in a bowl of warm water and then rinse again.

NOTE: Take care not to pour waxy water down the sink; I use a colander to strain the wax before tipping the water away. In fact the wax in the saucepan will solidify as it gets cold, and can easily be lifted from the pan and discarded. (It is not possible to re-use this wax as it is impregnated with water and soda.)

I use this method of completely removing wax very regularly when I am organizing the colour combinations in many of my batiks: in other words, I remove the wax half-way through my

TIP:

Remember to use a cheap non-steam iron for removing the wax as you do not want to spoil your best iron.

work, and then re-wax areas I wish to keep before introducing a new range of colours to areas no longer covered in wax. (*See* the step-by-step projects for details.)

DRY-CLEANING THE BATIK

Dry-cleaning is another method of removing the final traces of wax. You can use white spirit yourself for this, or take your ironed batik to be professionally dry-cleaned. If using white spirit, be careful to work in a well ventilated area, and to wear rubber gloves.

Put the white spirit into a bowl and lower the fabric into it. Cover completely for a minute or two, then remove and rinse. You will then need to wash your batik in warm soapy water to get rid of the smell of white spirit.

Remember that silk cannot be boiled, so after ironing it is essential to remove the remaining wax by a dry-cleaning process.

Presentation and Display

The final presentation of batik requires careful thought. What do you do with this flimsy piece of fabric, particularly if it is to be displayed on the wall? Many artists like to keep the fabric loose and flowing to emphasize the textile quality of the work. Batiks can be hung from above on a batten and allowed to float – they also work very well stretched on a wooden frame or stretcher with the fabric stapled or nailed round the frame, then set off with strips of beading round the edges. I have seen batiks lit from behind in specially constructed light-boxes, and they look wonderful. My own preferred method now is to have the batiks dry-mounted, a process whereby the fabric is bonded onto a backing card or hardboard under a hot press. Most picture framers offer dry-mounting, and this method means that the batik is kept permanently flat and ready to be framed with or without glass.

Clip frames are very useful as a quick and cheap method of displaying small pieces of batik.

BATIK ON PAPER

Although batik is generally associated with dyed fabrics, it is very simple and most effective to use wax and dyes on paper. Paper, like these natural fibres, is cellulose, and you can use almost any sort – newsprint or cartridge paper is excellent. If you hunt in specialist art shops you may be inspired to buy some of the beautiful absorbent Chinese paper, or papers incorporating interesting plant fibres.

Paper is exciting to work on because it is immediate and dries fast. It is a very useful first step in introducing batik in a teaching environment, particularly with children. Using exactly the same variety of tools, but not needing a frame to pin the paper on, wax is painted onto the paper to form a resist.

If you are working with children it is

A selection of home-made tools.

especially satisfying to encourage them first of all to make their own tools for applying the wax. Assemble a collection of corks, cardboard tubes and folded corrugated card, and then use scissors to cut interesting shapes in them. Masking tape is useful to hold cut shapes in place. Sponges can also be cut up to make good tools.

When you first put cardboard into the hot wax pot it tends to fizz, but although this is initially alarming it does not last

Using a bristle brush to re-wax dyed paper.

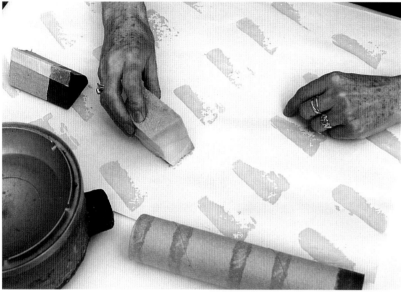

Using a sponge to make wax marks.

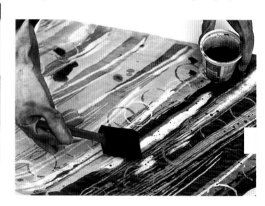

Painting Royal Blue Procion dye.

more than a few seconds. Shake off excess wax before printing the paper using these tools.

It is not essential when working on paper for the hot wax to penetrate thoroughly. This is because the work is not going to be dip-dyed, and because wax on paper cannot be crushed and cracked in quite the same way as wax on cotton fabric; therefore, interesting textured brush strokes are easy to achieve. When using a large bristle brush, for example, first shake off excess wax and then use repeat strokes across the paper without returning the brush to the wax pot. Even the most faint of wax

marks will resist the dyes. After the initial waxing, Procion dyes can then be painted in all shades of colour.

Procion dyes do not have to be fixed with the normal chemicals associated

A selection of greetings cards and wrapping paper.

with reactive dyes because paper, unlike fabric, is never going to be washed. You can wax and re-wax paper to build up layers of colour and then iron it out exactly like fabric. I suggest using paper batik to make greetings cards or very individual wrapping papers. Paper batik can also be combined with paper collage for particularly unusual results.

Paper Collage

Hot wax bonds paper together in much the same way as glue. Batik paper collage consists of overlapping layers of different sorts of dyed and bleached paper stuck down with wax. I make a point of not throwing away my scraps of dyed paper because I never know when they may prove useful. For example, I keep the kitchen towels I have previously used for blotting excess dye.

I have discussed bleach in a previous section, and it can also be used on paper, where it works particularly well. This is because it does not have to be rinsed off, as it does on cotton. Again, I must remind you to use bleach with caution, always wearing rubber gloves and being careful not to inhale the fumes of chlorine.

I find it fascinating to watch the effect of bleach on recently dyed paper. For example, try painting black dye all over a sheet of white newsprint, then dribble neat bleach onto the black. In an instant the most amazing reds, yellows and golds appear. You may wish to use this treated paper as the base for a collage, or perhaps tear it into smaller pieces for future use on top of another base sheet.

Another technique you can explore is to wax shapes onto coloured tissue paper and then to bleach the colour

Dribbling bleach onto dyed black paper.

Using a fine canting to wax lines on blue tissue paper.

Sponging bleach over waxed tissue paper.

away, leaving only the waxed lines.

These delicate traceries, when layered over other papers, will appear to float on the surface of the collage.

The possibilities inherent in paper collage are endless, the only limitations being those imposed by our own imagination. Almost anything can be incorporated. I have used coloured or lurex threads, bits of foil and even pencil sharpenings. When layering your materials, use a brush and hot wax to bond the paper. At first the materials can be adjusted and re-adjusted, but then as it cools the wax acts as a glue and the pattern sets. If you want to alter the design you just have to use a hot iron to melt the wax once more, thus allowing you to change the papers around.

Finally, when you are happy with the design, use a hot iron to spread the wax evenly across it, pushing the excess wax off the edges of the design onto the pad of newspaper underneath.

Paste Batik

Instead of wax, a flour paste or a mixture of flour and starch can be used as a resist. If you want to introduce children to resist dyeing, it may be helpful to try this method of batik to avoid any risk of burning from hot wax. The flour paste must be applied warm to fabric, and it needs to be allowed to dry slowly over a couple of days before the material can be dyed.

To make a flour paste: mix 1 tblsp rice flour, 1 tblsp white flour and ½ tblsp powdered laundry starch in a little cold water. Stir to remove lumps. Add 400 ml of water and boil in a small saucepan, stirring constantly. Let the paste boil until it becomes translucent (this usually takes between 5 and 10 minutes.).

Collage in progress, with iron.

Before starting to work, place a fat layer of newspaper under your fabric to soak up moisture from the paste as it dries; the fabric will need to be left to dry flat. The warm paste can be applied with brushes, spatulas or even piped on through an icing bag.

Left to dry, the fabric will get puckered; the paste layer then cracks if the fabric is pulled straight. Dyes applied by direct painting penetrate these cracks giving a batiked look. After leaving the dye to dry and fix for at least twelve hours, the fabric can be washed in warm water and the paste scraped off.

DESIGN AND INSPIRATION

From my own point of view I find it valuable to work from nature, which supplies us with an inexhaustible supply of inspirational possibilities. There are patterns and colour everywhere around you if you choose to look – at sunlight flickering through leaves, on water, on stones and on walls. Look at the shadows cast, and look for satisfying shapes. Collect interesting textural or coloured objects to stimulate design ideas. Pick up bark fragments, shells, pebbles, leaves and flowers, and really look at the textures. Collecting photos from papers and magazines can provide very useful reference material which can be a source of inspiration on a certain theme or image. It is important, though, to transform the source from which the images are taken into your own personal work. I take a lot of photographs, often in black and white, because again it is the tones and the order of tone that is important in batik.

In batik we are working from light to dark, so look particularly carefully at the light areas. A balance of light and shade is vital. The temptation with dye is to rush into the stronger, richer tones, but it is how strategically the pale colours are placed that will make the finished batik really work.

Batik design is not a precise art, and very often quite unexpected things happen. A colour, and one's perception of it, often changes depending on the colours that are juxtaposed to it. Dyes do not always produce the expected result, so you have to work with a degree of flexibility. And although it is possible to control crackle to some extent, there will always be an element of surprise. These surprises should be accepted as part of the process. It is also inevitable that, when working, you will get the odd splash of wax in the wrong place – sometimes it's a good idea to try to incorporate this into the design. The moral is: go with the flow!

Ultimately it will be the relationship of colour and shape, the balance of light and dark, which will give pleasure to the eye.

Project 1: Experimenting

Look on this first project as a play session, as above all a chance to make a mess! You don't have to do everything I suggest here, but I am trying to cover all the most basic techniques. The real point is to get you used to the feel of working with cantings and brushes, to get you to appreciate, for example, how speedily wax gets cold, and how to mix and apply the dyes. By the end of the session I hope that you will have created a useful sampler for future reference and will have begun to understand the full potential of batik.

WHAT YOU NEED:

- cotton lawn
- pencil
- frame
- drawing pins
- wax pot
- wax
- cantings
- bristle brush
- kettle
- yoghurt pots
- spoons
- washing-up bowl
- soft paintbrushes
- dyes and chemicals
- rubber gloves
- paper clips
- kitchen roll
- newspaper
- iron
- lining paper

and, as examples of how to get really experimental:

- washing-up brush
- toothbrush
- home-made stamp

I will be using a piece of cotton lawn approximately 25cm by 40cm; I find this a satisfactory shape and size and will be using it for most of the projects in this book. You can of course go smaller or very much larger; a lot will depend on the size of your frame.

Start by stretching the cotton onto the frame, pulling it from the corners and using drawing pins to hold it taut. Then divide the cotton into sections by drawing lines of hot wax across the fabric with a brush in order to make a series of squares.

Dividing the fabric into squares using a wax brush.

Experimenting with Tools

Treat each square as an experimental space in which to discover the effect of a variety of tools. Begin by making a variety of waxed marks, first of all with

Opposite: Sampler and tools used to create it.

cantings, experimenting to see the results you get with different sizes of spout. Dip each canting into the wax pot, wipe underneath with a tissue, and then try making spots, straight lines, wavy lines and zigzag lines; as you will discover, the marks will vary depending on the size of the spout of the canting used. Keep returning the canting to the wax pot to refill and reheat. Do not forget that the material will stay white where you draw the hot wax.

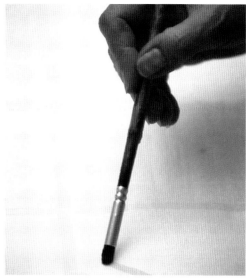

Experimental brush strokes using a variety of different brushes.

Using a kystka to wax zigzag lines.

Experimental brushstrokes using a variety of different brushes.

Next, try out bristle brushes of different widths and shapes. Instead of the relatively narrow lines drawn with the canting, you will find yourself painting broader shapes with the different brushes. You need to leave the brush in the wax pot for a moment or two in order to heat up. Again, you will find that the wax cools quickly while you are working, so dip the brush back in the hot wax pot frequently to make sure that the wax on your brush is hot enough to penetrate the fabric. Wax that sits on the surface of the fabric will not work as a resist to the dyes.

Using a washing-up brush to make waxed patterns.

Now try using a toothbrush or a washing-up brush. Put them into the wax pot and leave for a moment to heat up. Then shake off the excess wax to avoid blobs and apply to the fabric. Notice the interesting patterns that these household objects can achieve.

Toothbrush marks.

As a further experiment, and to give you an idea of the huge range of possibilities on offer, try making a home-made tool out of a paper towel. Fold it tightly, and then use scissors to cut the end to make it ragged. Put it in the wax pot for a moment, shake off the excess wax, and then stab it onto the cotton for a textured effect.

Using a paper towel to create textured marks.

Next I suggest that you fill in one space completely with hot wax so that you can experiment with etching. Paint the wax on with a broad brush and then scratch into it with a sharp tool, taking care not to make a hole in the fabric. As for the tool itself – it could be almost anything, but I find that an unfolded paperclip works particularly well, being small and delicate enough to avoid the risk of damaging the cotton

Etching with an unfolded paperclip.

Experimenting with Dyes

This initial playing with wax is vital to enable you to get a feel for the tools, but don't cover too much of your fabric with wax – you need to leave plenty of space between your waxed lines and shapes for colour to go. You will find that the wax dries on impact, so once you have decided that you have done enough you can start dyeing immediately – and that is the fun bit!

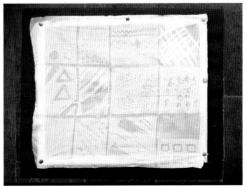

Sampler with the first waxing complete.

Make up a fix solution (*see* the recipe in the previous chapter), and half-fill each of four yoghurt pots with it. Add ¼ tsp of different coloured dye powder to each pot, and stir well. Take a soft paintbrush, dip it into the first dye and paint it onto a chosen area. Then do the same with a different dye on a different area. Wash your brush between each colour or use a different brush for each dye. As you will now see, the wax lines and shapes will form a resist and prevent the dye from running into the waxed areas.

Painting on the first colours.

Painting on the first colours.

Now comes one of the first problems you will encounter with batik: the drying time. It is vitally important to make sure that the material is bone dry before you begin to work on it again, because if the fabric is damp, the wax cannot penetrate and will sit on the

Completion of first dyeing process.

surface without forming a resist; the next dye will then creep under the wax from underneath and spoil the design. This is why you *must* allow time for the natural process of drying to take place before proceeding further. If you are in a hurry you can blot the dye with kitchen roll to absorb some moisture and speed up the drying process. If you are in a very great hurry a hair-drier blown across the fabric will work wonders.

When the fabric is at last bone dry, look at it and decide what you want to keep of the colour you have just dyed. Rewax each section using the various tools, this time painting the wax across some of the dyed colour in order to retain it. Note that wax has the effect of making the dyed fabric look darker than it will be when the wax is finally removed.

When sections of each area have been

Rewaxing certain sections to retain tho firct dye colour.

Re-waxing using a bristle brush

re-waxed, you can now paint the dyes again, this time using a different colour and painting on top of the previous colour; where there is no wax the dyes will combine, so that blue and yellow will make green, red and blue will make purple, and so on.

Wait until the material is completely

Painting on a stronger range of dyes.

More painting on of stronger dyes.

dry again. Then once more take a brush and a canting, and paint hot wax in order to keep those colours that you wish to retain in the areas where you wish to retain them.

Painting hot wax over the whole area so as to retain the colours.

INTRODUCING DIP-DYES

By this stage you should be getting a good idea of the basic batik process, so it might be time to introduce a little variation: a dip-dye. First of all, remove the material from the frame – it will be stiff with the cold wax. In order to create the crackle or marbled effect which gives batik its distinctive look, gently crush some of the waxed areas between your hands.

Do not scrunch it up too violently, but just gently rub some of the waxed areas between your fingers. Don't do this to the entire fabric, but be selective. Now you are ready to see the effect of the dip-dye process.

Cracking an area of wax to create the traditional marbling effect.

Pour ½ pint of fix into a washing-up sized bowl. Scoop out a little into a yoghurt pot. Dissolve 1 tsp of dye – I am using navy – in this little quantity of fix, and then pour it into the bowl with the rest of the fix. Put on your rubber gloves. Now gently lower your batik into the bowl of dye, making sure that all the fabric is covered.

Dip-dyeing.

Leave for 3 to 4 minutes, and then remove and hang on a line or a clothes airer so that it dries naturally in the air. Gently sponge off excess dye spots from both sides. The natural drying time should be up to 12 hours in order to make sure that the dyes have fixed into

Lowering the batik into a bath of dye for dip-dyeing.

Hanging to dry and sponging off excess droplets of dye.

the fabric. Rinse in cold water to remove any surplus surface dye, and dry again.

Now comes the moment of truth, when you take the wax off and reveal your design.

Finishing the Project

To remove the wax you need to work with an iron in a well ventilated space, preferably close to an extractor fan. It is a sensible precaution to protect your ironing board with a wad of newspaper. Cover the top layer with clean lining paper or, if you can find it, newsprint paper, and make a sandwich of your batik with more clean lining paper on top of it. Then simply iron the wax out of the batik and into the lining paper.

Discard the waxy sheets from above and below the batik, replace them with fresh ones, and continue to iron. Repeat this until most of the wax is melted out of the batik and the fabric feels soft. Then step back and admire your handiwork!

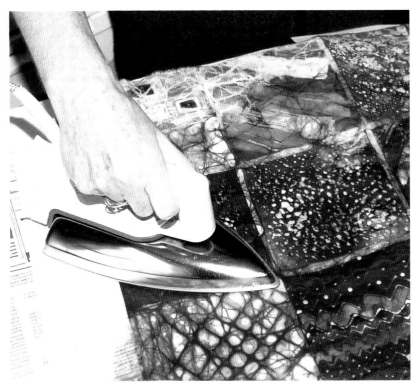

Ironing to remove more wax.

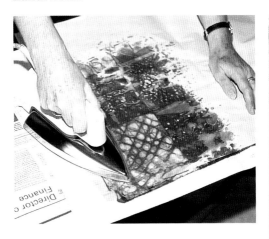

Initial ironing out of wax with the work sandwiched between layers of newsprint.

The final ironing.

Project 2: Leaf Project

This project involves painting on dyes using a wash technique, the design being strengthened and pulled together by a final dip-dye. I am using leaves of various shapes and sizes as inspiration.

WHAT YOU NEED:

- leaves
- cotton fabric
- pencil
- frame
- drawing pins
- wax pot
- wax
- bristle brushes
- fine canting
- kettle
- dyes and chemicals
- yoghurt pots
- washing-up bowl
- spoons
- rubber gloves
- paintbrushes and/or foam brushes
- kitchen roll
- iron
- newspaper
- lining paper

A selection of autumn leaves.

Preliminary sketches of autumn leaves.

First of all collect a variety of interesting leaves.

I recommend looking for bold-toothed shapes. Arrange the leaves in an overlapping design, and draw from life.

If you wish you can actually hold down the leaves on your cotton fabric and draw round their edges. Put the leaves beside you so that they are readily available for colour reference. When you are happy with the shapes you have drawn, start to think about where you want to keep the fabric white – perhaps to highlight some veining, or to outline one or other of the leaves, which is what I plan to do. Pin the fabric onto the frame and then take a canting and with hot wax begin to draw in the veins and the outlines you have decided to keep white.

Opposite: Framed picture of Leaves *in situ*

If you are in a hurry it is of course possible to speed up the drying process with the use of a hair dryer. The problem is that you must not melt the wax. Hold the dryer so that the air is blowing across the fabric, and not directly onto it.

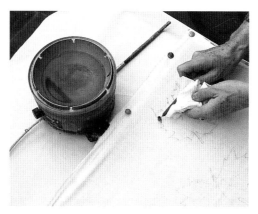

Using a canting to draw in veins and outlines.

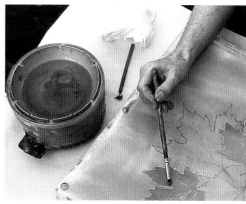

Blotting with kitchen roll.

This project proposes that you now wash three different dyes across your fabric so that there is some blending of the dyes into each other, but also areas in which the colours remain unblended. These first dyes will be pale. Mix up a fix solution (*see* previous recipe) and quarter-fill three yoghurt pots with this liquid. Working from light to dark, in the standard batik practice, your first dyes are weak: I suggest that you make up yellow, mahogany and blue. Add just ¼ tsp of dye powder to each yoghurt pot, and stir each one well.

The next step, before you begin to paint with the dyes, is to take a foam brush or a large painting brush and dampen your fabric with fix. This is because the dyes will only blend with each other if the fabric is wet. Once you have done this you can begin to use the dyes. Take the foam brush or the paintbrush and wash each of the pale dyes in turn across the fabric, not forgetting to rinse the brush between colours.

The idea, as you will now begin to appreciate, is to allow the colours to overlap and blend, thus increasing the richness and density of your batik. Blot dry, and then leave to dry naturally.

When the material is finally bone dry you can start waxing those areas where you wish to retain these subtle colours. I am using a bristle brush and have decided to completely fill in some of the leaf shapes.

Filling in some leaf shapes with a brush.

Now take up your canting once more and use it to outline other leaves and to draw in more veins.

You may find that your pencil lines have disappeared, and at this point it could be helpful to redraw some of the shapes.

When you are ready to dye again you will be adding stronger, darker tones.

Outlining with a canting.

Start by adding an extra ¼ tsp of dye powder to your existing yoghurt pot solutions. Then take two more yoghurt pots to mix two further shades – a navy dye and a red dye made with ½ tsp dye powder to half a yoghurt potful of fix solution. So now you will have medium strength solutions of the following colours: yellow, mahogany, blue, navy and red. Look at your leaves for reference and see what shades of green, yellow, red, orange and brown you want to try to match. Use more yoghurt pots to try combinations of your basic dyes.

As before, first dampen the fabric with fix, and then start painting the dyes onto it, using your paintbrush or foam brush and not forgetting to rinse the brush between dyes. Be bold and positive with your painting, and enjoy washing these mixes across your design. In particular take note of the way the colours change so rapidly – for me this moment is part of the great pleasure of batik.

Blot to remove excess dye.

Allow the batik to dry naturally and

Dabbing with kitchen roll to remove excess moisture.

then examine the dried leaf design carefully. Some of the pencil lines will almost certainly have disappeared, so redraw them where this has happened. Then, as before, you will have to decide which areas and lines of the new middle strength colours you wish to retain. Wax

Washing over a second range of dyes.

Waxing again to retain some of the leaf colours.

the outline of leaf shapes with a canting and, using the brush, fill in a few complete leaf shapes.

Now I am going to make up a brilliant blue dye using ½ tsp of dye in a yoghurt pot half-full of fix. This time there will be no need to dampen the fabric with fix, because I am just using a single dye and it doesn't need to blend with other colours. I will now wash this brilliant blue over the whole fabric.

Blotting with kitchen roll to remove excess moisture.

Washing over a brilliant blue dye.

Washing over a brilliant blue dye.

The next step is to blot to remove excess dye, and then the batik is left to dry naturally. There is now only one step left in the dyeing process: the final dip-dye. First, though, you must wax all over the areas of newly painted colour that you wish to keep. In this project I am going to wax completely the individual leaves, while leaving fine lines unwaxed between the various

shapes. It is these lines which will pick up the final dye and give definition to the design.

If you want to have cracking or

Waxing more leaves, leaving fine lines between the shapes.

marbling you will need to select which areas will be treated in this way; these you will rub gently between your fingers, so as to break down the wax. Take the work off the frame and gently crunch a few areas of wax. Don't overdo this, though – I find that a limited amount of cracking has much more impact than an overall, unselective treatment.

To check on this, hold the material up to the light to inspect the amount of cracking. If you have let the wax break

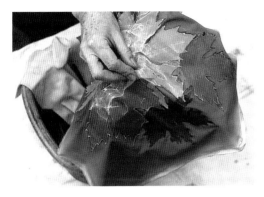

Gently crushing the fabric as the batik is lowered into the dye bath.

down too much you can, if you choose, paint more hot wax over those areas. This will melt the over-cracked wax and thereby correct the mistake.

Now mix up a dip-dye. Put ½ pint of fix solution in a washing-up bowl. Scoop out ½ yoghurt pot full of this solution and add 1 to 2 tsp of dye powder, depending on the final strength of colour required. I am using mahogany dye. Don't forget to wear rubber gloves when dip-dyeing. Place the batik in the dye solution and agitate it to make sure that all the areas of the batik have come in contact with the dye. You should now leave it in the solution for 3 to 4 minutes.

Finally remove the batik and hang to

Dip-dyeing in a mahogany dye.

dry, sponging off any excess drops of dye; leave to dry naturally for at least 12 hours.

Hanging to dry and sponging off excess droplets of dye.

I now find it advisable to rinse the fabric in cold running water in order to remove any excess dye which it has been unable to absorb. Then at last it is time to remove the wax from the fabric by ironing – see the method described in the previous project.

The project is now complete.

Project 3: Dip-Dyeing Project

WHAT YOU NEED:

- cotton
- pencil
- frame
- drawing pins
- wax pot
- wax
- cantings
- brushes
- kitchen roll
- dyes and chemicals
- yoghurt pots
- baby bath, or washing-up bowl
- rubber gloves
- washing line
- pegs
- sponge

The idea of this project is to follow a simple sequence of colours using a dip-dye process in which the whole fabric is dipped into the dye solution for each colour change. This is the traditional method. You will appreciate that the first dye bath determines the direction in which the colour scheme is to develop. If, for example, you start by dipping your fabric in a yellow dye, there is no possibility of achieving a blue overdye, simply because by adding blue dye to yellow you would get green. It is therefore essential to have a very clear view of what exactly you are hoping to achieve.

I have chosen, as a design subject, a scene inspired by a detail on an Indian woodcut: figures and their reflection in water. The dyes I have selected are mahogany, yellow and blue.

First of all draw the basic structure of the design in pencil onto your fabric. Once you are satisfied with your drawing, stretch the fabric onto a frame. Now study the image. What is to be kept white? I have decided to keep the background white and so I wax it carefully, using a canting to outline the figures and a brush to fill in larger areas.

Waxing to keep the background white.

I wax the watery areas with less defined brush strokes in order to indicate a broken reflection.

When everything that is to remain white is covered in wax, it is time for the first dye bath.

Make up a fix solution and pour ½ pint into a suitable container: a washing-up bowl or a baby bath. It is wasteful to make up unnecessarily large quantities of dye – you just need enough dye solution to cover the fabric. It does not

Opposite: Dip dyeing: close up of water buffalo picture.

have to be totally submerged. For this project my piece of cotton is not large, and ½ pint of fixative solution is enough.

Scoop out a yoghurt pot half-full of fix. Add ¼ tsp of mahogany dye powder. Stir well, and add to the fix in the bowl. Take the fabric off the frame and, wearing rubber gloves, lower it into the dye bath and leave for two minutes, turning it frequently to make sure that the dye is reaching all parts of the fabric.

The first dip-dye into a pale mahogany bath.

Then lift the fabric out and hang it on a line or a clothes airer to dry. Sponge off drops of excess dye to prevent it collecting on the waxed areas.

Hanging to dry and sponging off excess dye.

Everything that is not covered in wax is now pale pink. When dry, pin the fabric back onto the frame. Again, look hard at your design and decide what is to remain pink. I have decided to keep the figures pink and so I wax them

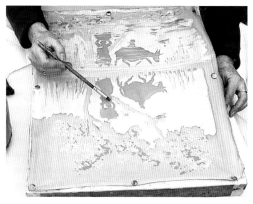

Waxing to keep the figures pink.

carefully using a brush.

I also wish to indicate leaves in the tree and so, using a screwed-up paper towel, I am going to dab on a little wax here; these marks will also now stay pink. At this point check for waxed areas of white background which may have been cracked too much, and retouch with hot wax. This will have the effect of retaining some pale pink marbling lines.

Now it is time for the next dye bath. Pour ½ pint of fix into a clean bowl and

Dip-dyeing into a green dye.

scoop out a yoghurt pot half-full of fix. Add ¼ tsp of blue dye and ¼ tsp of yellow dye to create a green. Stir and add to the bowl.

Remove the fabric from the frame and, having put on your rubber gloves, lower it into the green dye. Keep it there for two minutes, turning it as before.

Then lift the fabric out and hang it to dry. Again, blot any excess dye with a sponge. You will now see that your batik has white, pink and green areas.

Waxing the grass shapes and the leaf shapes so they remain green.

Hanging to dry and sponging off excess dye.

When the fabric is dry, re-pin it to the frame. This time I intend to wax so as to keep the grass shapes and the leaf shapes green. I use both a brush and a canting to achieve the marks I want.

Now for the next dye: this will be mahogany again, but in a stronger ratio. This time add 1 tsp of mahogany dye to ½ pint of fix. Remove your batik from the frame and gently crush some of the stiff waxed areas between your finger and thumb; the dark dye will penetrate these cracks and encourage the marbling effect.

Gently crushing some of the waxed background between finger and thumb.

Wearing rubber gloves, lower your batik into the mahogany dye; turn frequently, as before. Remove after 2–3

TIP:

If you feel that the dye is too strong you can rinse the batik in clean water. As the dyes have not yet fixed into the fabric they can be diluted this way.

Dip-dyeing in mahogany.

Hanging to dry and sponging off excess dye.

minutes, by which time the dye will have covered all the unwaxed areas and penetrated the cracks.

Then hang the fabric on a line to dry, and again sponge off the excess droplets of dye trapped in the cracked wax.

When the fabric is dry, re-pin it onto the frame and examine all the waxed areas. The last dye acts mainly as definition to the shapes and is very important in terms of design. For instance, it may be that you do not want the cracks that you have to be any darker; if so, you need to ensure that they are now covered with hot wax in order to retain them as they are.

In this particular design I use a brush to paint hot wax onto the tree trunk in such a way that I leave a fine line unwaxed between the trunk and the white background. This line is where the final dye will go and will give the trunk definition. I also wax more leaf shapes and more grass shapes to retain the deeper pink.

Waxing the tree trunk with a brush.

The final dye will be the strongest. Wearing rubber gloves, mix ½ tsp of blue dye, ½ tsp of yellow dye and ½ tsp of mahogany dye into ½ pint of fixative. Stir well, then lower the batik into the bowl.

Dip-dyeing in the final dark colour.

Agitating the batik for 2 minutes in the dye bath.

Leave for 2 minutes, turning to make sure that the dye reaches all parts of the fabric. Then lift the fabric out and hang it up to dry. Again, sponge off any excess droplets.

The design is now complete. After leaving the finished batik to dry for twelve hours, rinse it in clear water to remove any excess dye which the fabric is unable to absorb. Then dry once more and iron to finish.

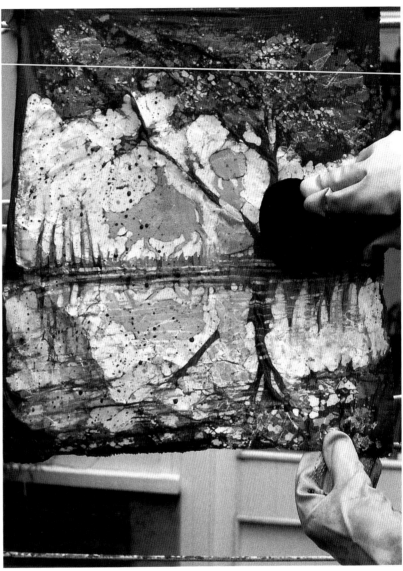

Hanging the fabric to dry for the last time.
The final sponge.

Project 4: Boiling Out at a Half Way Stage

Aim:

To introduce a new range of colours, and to add further subtlety to the process.

WHAT YOU NEED:

- cotton
- pencil
- frame
- drawing pins
- wax pot
- wax
- cantings
- wax brushes
- kitchen roll
- dyes: a range, including brilliant blue, royal blue, brilliant red, brilliant yellow, mahogany, chrome yellow
- chemicals
- paint brushes
- yoghurt pots
- an *old* saucepan
- washing soda crystals
- washing-up liquid
- washing-up bowl
- tongs

I have chosen as a subject some *Clematis* 'Jackmanii' flowers and leaves which were growing in my garden amongst variegated ivy. The project will show you how to block out areas with wax, keeping them white initially, but enabling bright dye to be introduced at a half-way stage once the wax has been removed by boiling. Areas will then be re-waxed allowing an interesting overlapping of dyes.

First of all, draw your design in pencil onto cotton.

Drawing the clematis design in pencil.

Then stretch the fabric onto a frame and fasten with drawing pins. Use a brush to wax the shape of the petals, leaving a thin line between them. I am keeping the petals white for the time being. I then use a fine canting to wax a few stamens in the centre of each flower.

Waxing the shape of the petals.

Opposite: Clematis and leaves.

Mix up a fix solution. Take a yoghurt pot half-full of fix; add ½ tsp chrome yellow dye, and stir. Take another yoghurt pot half-full of fix; add ¼ tsp brilliant blue dye, and stir. Use a foam brush to dampen your fabric with the fix solution. Use the same brush to wash the yellow dye over the design.

While the fabric is wet, use another brush to splash the blue dye over certain areas. Again, be bold, and don't be afraid of a vigorous approach to the design. Blot and dry.

Splashing blue dye over certain areas. The blue on top of yellow makes green.

Washing yellow dye over the design.

Blotting dry.

Washing yellow dye over the design.

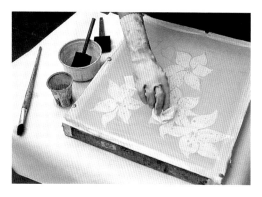

Blotting excess yellow dye with kitchen roll.

Waxing the outlines of the palest leaves.

Then use a brush to wax the palest colours of the leaves, and a canting to draw the veins and to draw in more stamens. Leave spaces for the stems.

Using a canting to draw in the stamens.

Take ½ yoghurt pot of fix and add ¼ tsp brilliant yellow dye and ½ tsp brilliant blue dye to make a green. Stir well. Dampen the fabric again with the

Painting on green dye.

Painting on green dye.

fix solution. Paint on the green dye, then blot and dry. As you will see, for the next stage it is important that the fabric is fully dry.

When the fabric is ready, take a yoghurt pot half-full of fix, add ¼ tsp mahogany dye, and stir. This is the time for a delicate approach. Using a dry paintbrush, carefully paint the dye very sparingly to indicate the tracery of stems.

Using mahogany on a dry paintbrush to indicate the stems.

If the fabric is dry, these lines of dye will not spread far. Once you have finished painting the stems it is important to be sure that the dyes are fully fixed and fast, so the fabric must be left to dry and fix for at least twelve hours.

The next stage is the boiling part.

Pouring washing soda crystals into soapy water in an old saucepan.

Take a large old saucepan. Pour ½ cup of washing soda crystals into the saucepan, add a generous squirt of washing-up liquid and then enough hot water to come half way up the inside of the saucepan. Put on the cooker to boil. When the water is boiling, take your waxy batik and lower it into the saucepan. Bring the water back to the boil, and agitate the fabric with tongs or a suitable implement.

Removing the fabric with an old knife.

Lowering the waxy batik into the saucepan.

Taking the saucepan over to the sink.

Bringing the water to the boil.

Boil for one minute, then remove the fabric and, wearing rubber gloves, rinse in warm water.

Do not pour this waxy water straight down the sink, but use a colander to strain it first. Meanwhile, the solution in the saucepan can be left to cool. When cold, the wax will have risen to the surface and can then be removed easily.

Rinsing the fabric in warm water to remove all the wax superficially adhering to the fibres.

Do not attempt to re-use it as it is impregnated with soda and water; it should be discarded. Give the fabric a shake to remove any wax that may be clinging superficially to the surface. It will now be free of all wax and can be hung up to dry.

When your fabric has dried out, re-pin it to the frame, take a good look at it, and decide which areas of colour you want to retain. Use a brush or a canting to wax the stems to keep them brown. By now I hope that you will have a good idea as to your preference for a given tool in a given situation. Wax the leaves to keep them yellow and green. Use a canting to wax the delicate stamens and keep them white and yellow.

Re-waxing the leaves with a brush.

Re-waxing the stamens with a canting.

Make up a fix solution. Next, choose the colour you want for the flowers. My clematis petals are two-toned, mauve and purple, so I shall first make up a mauve dye by adding ¼ tsp brilliant red and ¼ tsp brilliant blue to ½ yoghurt pot of fix. With any mix, stir well, and adjust the dye strength to get exactly the right

shade, adding more dye or more fix as required. Use a foam brush to dampen the fabric with fix, and then use the same brush to wash the mauve dye over the whole surface.

Painting a mauve dye over the whole surface with a foam brush.

Mauve dye painted over the whole design.

Waxing to retain mauve on the petals.

When dry, use a brush to wax more of the leaf shapes – by now a slightly different shade of green. Wax to keep the centre of each petal mauve.

Waxing to retain mauve on the petals and on some green leaves.

Make up a purple dye by adding ¼ tsp of brilliant red dye to ¾ tsp royal blue dye. Paint the colour over the whole design. Then blot and dry.

Painting purple dye with a foam brush.

Painting purple dye with a foam brush

Blotting with kitchen roll to remove excess dye.

When dry, wax each petal carefully, making sure that you leave a fine line between the petals for one more last dye. Finish waxing all the leaves. The last dye will be a dip-dye and will give definition to the design as well as a chance to have some cracking on the leaves and petals.

Finishing all the waxing of the petals and leaves.

Take your batik off its frame and gently crush some of the waxed areas. Now make up a fix solution. Then scoop out ½ yoghurt pot of this fix and add 1 heaped tsp mahogany dye to it; stir, then pour it into ½ pint of fix in a different bowl. Put on your rubber gloves. Gently lower your batik into this bowl of dye, making sure that all the fabric is covered. Encourage the dye to go into the cracks by rubbing the fabric gently with your fingers. Leave for 3 to 4 minutes, then remove it and hang it to dry in the air. Gently sponge off the excess dye spots from both sides. Mahogany is a warm tone and, as you may have noticed, is a favourite of mine for a final dye.

Hanging to dry after the final dip-dye in mahogany. Sponging off the excess droplets of dye.

Allow the fabric to dry naturally overnight or for at least twelve hours so that the dyes are definitely fixed. Rinse in cold water to remove the excess dye; dry again, and iron to finish.

Project 5: Cushion Covers

In this project we shall be using bleach to discharge – that is, remove colours from – black cotton velvet.

WHAT YOU NEED:

- two pieces of black cotton velvet or black lawn 50cm by 50cm
- frame
- drawing pins
- wax pot
- wax
- cantings
- brushes
- kitchen roll
- washing-up bowl
- strong rubber gloves
- bleach
- vinegar
- dyes: I am using brilliant red, brilliant yellow, mahogany

The aim of this project is to experiment with bleach, but more importantly, to show how to retain a really strong black as a colour. Unlike other Procion dyes, black seems to be unstable and has a tendency to wash out. Bleach will be used to discharge or remove colour from unwaxed areas so that further colours can be added.

I am working on black cotton velvet because the finished fabric has a soft richness ideal for a cushion cover. But a word of warning: I have found that some black cotton velvet bleaches out better than others. Because of this it is worth testing a small piece of fabric by waxing a simple series of wax stripes and then dipping the sample into a bleach solution. You may find that it will bleach out to beige or yellow, or it may remain a pink or rust colour. Black lawn, by contrast, seems to be more regular in its reaction and usually bleaches out to a pale cream. The point of checking the colour is to determine the range of dyes which you can use to over-dye the bleached areas.

Samples of bleaching out on strips of black cotton velvet and black cotton lawn.

Opposite: Cushion on chair *in situ*.

First, decide on a design and mark it out on one piece of black velvet using tailor's chalk or a white marking pencil.

Marking out a design with a white pencil.

My design is abstract. Pin the fabric onto the frame with drawing pins with the velvet side uppermost. Use a medium-stiff brush, and a canting with a medium-sized spout to paint hot wax onto the fabric. Remember you are waxing to keep the black colour, and

these lines will play a vital role in the finished design. It is very important to make sure that the hot wax really penetrates the fabric, and it may be necessary to wax and then re-wax the design to overcome this. Check the reverse to see if the wax has penetrated.

Next, remove the waxed fabric from the frame. Wearing strong rubber gloves, make up a bleach solution in a washing-up bowl. Cotton velvet is resilient, so the solution can be as strong as 1 part bleach to 1 part water.

If working on black lawn I recommend a weaker solution of bleach. Be careful not to inhale the fumes.

Immerse the black fabric in the bleach solution and agitate, ensuring complete evenness, for about five minutes. Check to see if all the black dye has discharged. Add a little neat bleach if necessary.

Tipping bleach into a washing-up bowl.

Waxing with a brush to keep the fabric black.

Immersing the fabric in a bleach solution.

Rinse thoroughly in plenty of running water. When the fabric no longer smells of bleach, place it in a bowl containing a neutralizing solution of half vinegar and half water. This vinegar rinse is to stop any further damage to the fibres.

Neutralizing with a vinegar rinse.

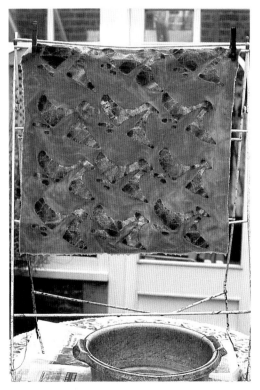

Hanging to dry after rinsing thoroughly in cold water.

Then rinse again in more cold water, and hang to dry in a warm area overnight. Cotton velvet takes a long time to dry.

When dry, re-pin onto the frame. This time wax to retain some of the bleached colour, which may look a shade of pink/beige.

Waxing with a canting to keep the bleached colour.

Make up a fix solution. Using three yoghurt pots half-filled with fix, make up three different dyes. Add ½ tsp of brilliant red to one pot, ½ tsp of

Painting dyes on in random splashes.

Painting dyes on in random splashes.

mahogany to another pot, and ½ tsp of brilliant yellow to the third pot. Stir all the pots, then dampen the fabric with fix. Wearing rubber gloves, paint these dyes onto specific areas not covered with wax, according to the design you have planned – or, as I am doing, in random splashes of colour.

Dry overnight. Removing the wax from the velvet may appear to be a daunting task; I find that the best way to achieve this is to boil it out and then to finish it off by using white spirit as a solvent. When boiling out make sure that you add plenty of washing soda crystals and plenty of washing-up liquid to the hot water in the pan. For this project I used ½ eggcup of washing-up liquid and 1 cupful of washing soda crystals,

Boil rapidly for 1–2 minutes, then rinse thoroughly in warm water. I found that there was still a vestige of wax in the velvet fabric even after boiling, and to remove this completely I placed the fabric in a small bowl containing white spirit. Do this in a well ventilated area. Then rinse very thoroughly in plenty of

soapy water until the smell of white spirit has disappeared. Hang to dry.

This method of removing wax does inevitably mean that you lose a considerable amount of dye. My cushion cover has retained black, but has lost a lot of the vibrancy of the red dyes. The bleached areas look very pale, though, which I like. Because it is less easy to predict results, this is a very experimental project, and please treat it as such.

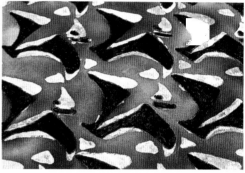

Close-up of the cushion cover design after the wax has been removed by boiling and by immersion in white spirit.

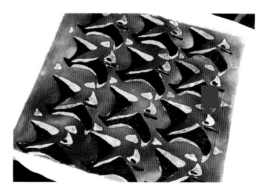

The finished cushion cover design.

You can, of course, take the fabric to your local dry cleaners if you decide not to try white spirit yourself.

Make the fabric up into a cushion cover using the other piece of black velvet for the reverse side.

Project 6: Landscape Project

This project will use and refine the techniques learned in the preceding chapters. Batik is a valid art form and I personally use batik largely as a medium for producing landscapes as wall hangings and as framed pictures. This is an example of how I set about it.

WHAT YOU NEED:

- cotton
- pencil
- frame
- drawing pins
- wax pot
- wax
- cantings
- brushes
- paper towels
- rubber gloves
- dyes and chemicals
- kettle
- bowls
- yoghurt pots
- spoons

Although I often use photographs as a starting point for many of my landscape designs, I also like to work from charcoal sketches or watercolour washes. In this project I am taking as my subject the River Dovey in Powys, sketched in late evening. I am making it a study in shades of pink, grey and silver, and I shall be using a restricted palette of dyes in a very painterly fashion. Use this project as a guide, but feel free to be flexible and to

Preliminary charcoal sketch of the River Dovey in Powys.

alter it to suit your own colour schemes.

By now you should have more of a feel for colour, and be ready to experiment. I am using a black dye which when diluted and weak makes a useful grey colour. I shall be both hand-painting and dip-dyeing.

Waxing highlights on the water.

Cracking the wax over the sun.

Draw in pencil the rough design on cotton, and then pin the fabric onto the frame with drawing pins. Begin this project by deciding which areas you want to remain white. Wax the highlights on the water, and a little where the sun is setting. Crack this area of wax over the sun.

Make up a fix solution. Scoop out enough to half-fill three yoghurt pots. Add ⅛ tsp of dye to each pot. I am using brilliant yellow, mahogany and black. Dampen the fabric with fixative.

The first colour wash is very pale. Start with the sun: place the pale yellow dye carefully in the sky and rub into the cracks in the sun. Paint yellow in the water beneath the reflected sun. Use the weak mahogany and black dyes to suggest a misty but slightly menacing sky. Paint these dyes strategically over the fabric.

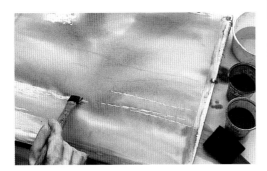

The first colour wash.

Leave to dry naturally. When bone dry, wax the areas of colour in the sky which you want to retain. Also wax some of the silvery river colour. Use a canting to pick out light areas through the trees. Crack the wax again over the sun.

Waxing the silvery river colour.

Painting slightly stronger dyes strategically over the design.

Opposite: Landscape painting with original sketch.

Make up a fix and use the same range of dyes but make them up a bit stronger: I suggest ¼–½ tsp of dye to each ½ yoghurt pot of fix.

Dampen the fabric with fix. Paint the yellow over the sun, rubbing it into the cracked wax. Paint a little mahogany into these same cracks. Paint mahogany and black strategically to build up the clouds and river bed. Then blot to remove the excess dye and droplets from the surface of the wax.

Painting slightly stronger dyes strategically over the design.

Blotting to remove excess dye.

When dry, wax to retain these colours, paying particular attention to covering the sky completely so as to retain the variety of colours. Use a big bristle brush for this process, and a smaller brush to carefully edge the area between hill and sky.

Waxing between the sky and the hill to give a sharp edge.

Now you are going to dip-dye the whole fabric in one colour. Make up a pink/grey dye using ½ tsp mahogany, ⅛ tsp brilliant red and ½ tsp black. Take the fabric off the frame, carefully crack some of the areas of wax, and dip-dye in 1 litre of fix. Leave in the dye bath for 2 minutes.

Dip-dyeing in a grey/pink dye bath.

Hang to dry, and sponge to remove the excess droplets of dye. When completely dry, rc-pin your fabric onto the frame.

Leaving to fix in the dye bath.

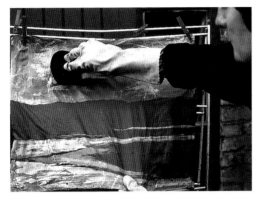

Hanging to dry, and sponging off the excess droplets from the wax.

Wax a section of hillside and more of the river bed. At this stage it is very important to check the amount of cracking and to stop the wax becoming too broken up. The composition of the wax mixture is very important. If you have too much paraffin wax in the mixture you may find that the wax cracks excessively and even lifts off the fabric. I want some crackle, but I do not want the design obscured by too much dark veining. So at this stage I check for cracks. Use a bristle brush loaded with really hot wax to press down to melt through any broken wax on your design. Keep returning the brush to the wax pot so that the wax on the brush is kept hot. Do not forget that every time fresh dye is added, the colours get darker and stronger. Bear this in mind, and wax so

as to keep some veining in these subtle shades, and to leave some other veining to pick up subsequent darker dyes.

Waxing to retain a section of hillside.

Waxing to retain a section of hillside.

Make up a slightly stronger dye solution using a mix of the same dyes to make a subtle but slightly different colour of hillside. To make a difference I am varying the colour by adding ⅛ tsp more black powder to the original mix and introducing ⅛ tsp brilliant yellow dye. Dampen the fabric with fix, and wash this dye over the whole fabric using a soft paintbrush.

Washing over the next dye solution.

Washing over the next dye solution.

Dry thoroughly, then wax another section of hillside. Using a tool made from a rolled up and cut kitchen paper towel, wax to suggest light coming through the trees. Check again whether the cracking is becoming too dominant. Re-wax any broken areas in the sky.

Using a tool made from a kitchen paper towel rolled and cut.

Waxing another area of hillside.

Waxing the area below the trees.

Make up another slight variation of the same dyes. I suggest that you make up a very similar mix as for the previous stage, but add just a little more dye powder so that the tone will be marginally darker. Experiment, and test your colour on a corner of the fabric to check whether it is sufficiently different. I am all for subtlety, but you do need to make sure each dye adds something significant. Dampen your fabric and wash this colour over the design. Blot with kitchen roll to remove any excess dye, and allow to dry naturally.

The next dye being washed over the design.

Blotting with kitchen roll.

When completely dry, wax the third area of hillside, being sure to leave uncovered everything that you want to pick up the last dark colour. It is a good idea to examine the back of the fabric from time to time. You have been working on the front and it may appear to be well waxed, but occasionally the wax may not have penetrated fully. Looking on the back of the fabric gives a much better idea as to whether there are areas that have not been completely covered and that need re-waxing.

The final waxing before the last dark dye.

The final waxing before the last dark dye.

TIP:

Before a final dye, after checking that everything to be retained is covered in wax, also check that the cracking has not become too dominant. Melt with really hot wax to avoid any further veining.

The last dramatic dye.

Make up a fix solution. Add ½ tsp black and ½ tsp mahogany to a yoghurt pot half-filled with fix. Wash over the design. This is the last dye and it should be dark and dramatic; it will penetrate any spaces left between wax shapes. This line of dark dye offers useful definition to the design.

Allow to dry for twelve hours. Rinse to remove the excess dye. Dry again, and then iron to finish.

The last dark dye before it is blotted.

Project 7:
Silk Chiffon Scarf

A silk chiffon scarf dyed using ferrous sulphate, fast black K-salt and indigo.

This project introduces a new range of dip-dye possibilities for the adventurous. Ferrous sulphate, bought from chemists in its green crystalline form, can be used to dye silk a lovely shade of yellow. When soda is added, the yellow colour turns to gold.

Fast black K-salt is obtainable as a brown powder from specialist suppliers, and dyes silk in shades of pink. If or when soda is added to a K-salt solution, the dye colour is again altered, this time to shades of brownish pink. Neither ferrous sulphate nor K-salt react well on cotton fibres, but I often choose to use them on silks of all weights because they offer such a fresh range of subtle tones.

Indigo, as previously discussed, is a vat dye creating shades of blue, and dyes both silk and cotton equally well.

WHAT YOU NEED:

- silk chiffon in scarf length
- long thin wooden frame
- silk pins or drawing pins
- wax pot
- wax
- cantings
- bristle brushes
- rubber gloves
- ferrous sulphate crystals
- K-salt powder
- prepared indigo vat
- washing soda crystals
- bowls
- buckets
- spoons
- measuring jug
- sponge
- washing line and pegs
- white spirit
- iron
- newsprint
- newspaper

Ferrous sulphate crystals and K-salt powder with small mixing bowls.

First stretch and pin your scarf onto the frame. Wax the initial design so as to keep areas of silk white, using both canting and brush. I am using a theme of pebble shapes.

Initial waxing, to keep some of the original white of the silk chiffon.

Make up a ferrous sulphate solution. My recipe is very simple: mix one heaped dessertspoon of ferrous sulphate crystals in a pint of cold water and stir to dissolve. Please note that this solution will only last for one day. Take the silk off the frame, very carefully, and, wearing rubber gloves, dip it into the solution.

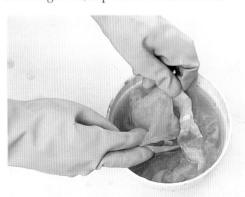

Dipping the silk into a ferrous sulphate solution.

Leave for a couple of minutes. Then remove the silk and hang it on a washing line to dry. The silk will now be a pale yellow.

Hanging to dry.

When the fabric is dry, repin the scarf to the frame. Use a brush to wax again, this time retaining some of the new yellow colour.

Using a brush to retain some pale yellow colour.

Remove the silk from the frame and put the scarf into a soda solution made up from a dessertspoon of washing soda crystals dissolved in a pint of water. Remember, as always, to wear rubber gloves. Leave the silk submerged for one minute.

Submerging the silk in a washing soda solution.

The fabric will initially turn green, but hang it up once more and the colour will change to gold as the fabric dries out in the air.

Hanging to dry.

After drying, rinse the scarf in cold water to wash the soda out of the silk fibres. Hang up to dry once more and then re-pin onto the frame. Using a brush and a canting wax to retain some of the gold colour.

Waxing to retain some of the gold colour.

Now prepare your K-salt solution. My recipe is as follows:

- Mix ½ tsp of K-salt with a little cold water and stir into a paste.
- Pour this paste into a pint of cold water. This quantity will produce a very pale pink dye.
- Increase the quantity of K-salt if you want to make a stronger pink.
- Always use cold water, as hot water will destroy this dye.
- Remove the scarf from the frame and, wearing rubber gloves, dip it into the K-salt solution.

Dipping the scarf into K-slat solution.

I have made up a fairly strong solution for my particular design. Leave the fabric in the solution for five minutes and then hang up to dry.

Opposite: The finished scarf.

Hanging to dry.

When the scarf is dry, re-pin it once more to the frame and wax again, this time to retain some of the rusty pink colour. By now you will find that a lot of the wax has cracked, so at this stage it could be a good idea to rewax most of the design in order to stop it getting too broken.

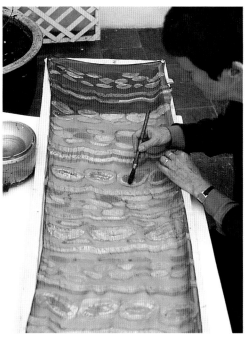

Waxing to retain some rusty pink, and re-waxing other areas of the design which have become very cracked.

I plan now to dip the scarf into a final indigo vat. I could have put the scarf into yet another soda solution which would have altered the pink tones, but I've decided that this scarf is quite busy enough!

Find out about indigo dyeing by reading the section in my earlier chapter on the Batik process. For the sake of the photograph I have taken some indigo solution and put it into a small bucket, but care must still be taken to eliminate oxygen from the solution. Remember that the fabric needs to be wet before

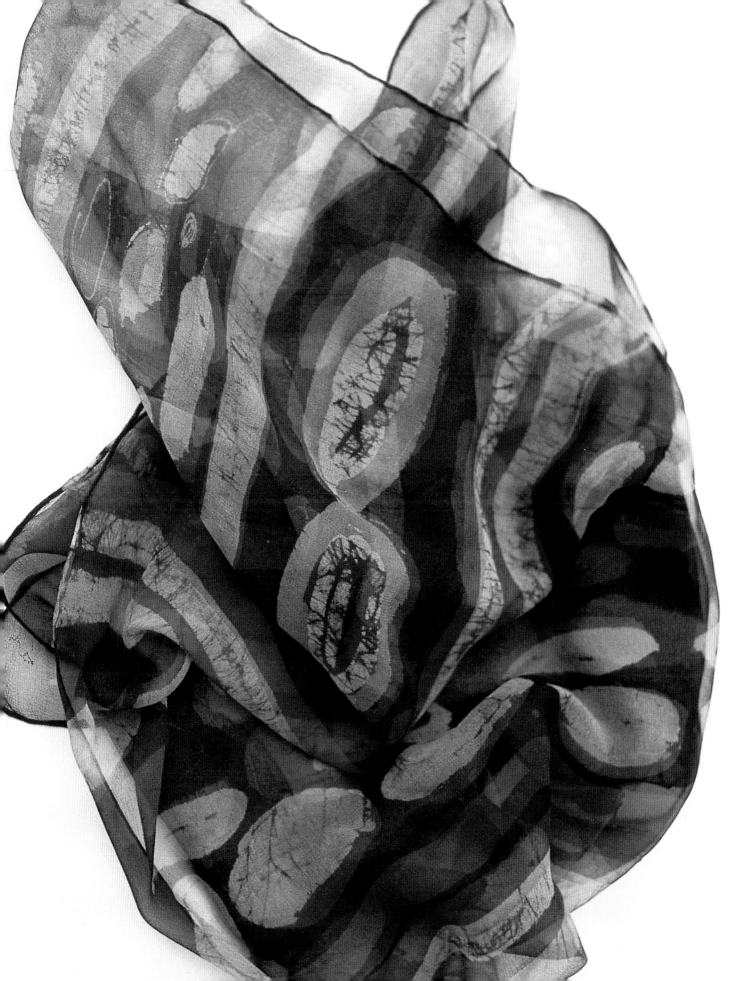

immersing it in the indigo, and it really is essential to wear rubber gloves, since indigo dyeing is a very messy and smelly process.

Dipping the scarf into a bucket of indigo.

Cover the bucket and leave the scarf submerged for 5–10 minutes, then remove it and hang it up to dry. The indigo leaves a green bloom on the fabric which needs to be sponged off.

The blue colour develops as the oxygen reacts with the silk fibres. At this stage it will be virtually impossible to see what the design will be like – you need to be fairly philosophical! The wax will have cracked considerably and there will be much blue veining. Leave to oxidize and to dry. Then rinse thoroughly to remove any excess indigo before hanging up to dry once more. The next step is to iron between lots of lining paper to remove the excess wax.

When you have removed a reasonable amount of wax, immerse the scarf in a pot of white spirit. This process is excellent for dissolving out the residue of wax, but you must take care not to inhale the fumes from the white spirit. I recommend doing this part of the process in the open air. The scarf will now smell of the white spirit, so to get rid of this you will now need to rinse it in warm water containing a generous squirt of washing-up liquid. Rinse again and then iron once more with a clean, non-waxy iron to reveal the beauty of the dyed chiffon.

Although this process may seem time-consuming, you will find that you have produced a unique, subtle and beautiful piece of work.

Hanging to dry.

5 Gallery

Hetty van Boekhout

**Changing Seasons
(100 x 90cm)**
Batik on Chinese
paper using Procion
dyes, bleach and
spray technique,
working on both
sides of the paper.

Hetty van Boekhout

Escape (90 x 80cm)
Collage batik on tissue
and cartridge paper using
Procion dyes and bleach.

Jane Christie

Fish Bones (46 x 46cm)
Batik on cotton, using
Procion dyes.

Sheila Cook

**Le Spectre de la Rose
(43 x 68.5cm)**
Soft hanging, using
Procion dyes on silk.

Gill Curry

Life? Or Theatre?
Lino print and batik on
tissue paper.

Diana Fenney

Girl with Pansies
Batik on paper and
tissue paper.

Diana Fenney

Mother Teresa
Batik on paper and tissue
paper.

Helen Heery

Batik silk/viscose scarves
with georgette silk lining,
using ferrous sulphate,
k-salt and indigo as dyes.

Ruth Holmes

**Timoleague Abbey,
West Cork (68 x 54cm)**
Batik on cotton.

Jenny Morse

Untitled (20 x 20cm)
Batik on paper, silk and cotton.

Rosi Robinson

Drive for Four (79 x 64cm)
Batik on cotton.

Rosi Robinson

Rooftops (80 x 64cm)
Wax resist and discharge
technique on Japanese
paper.

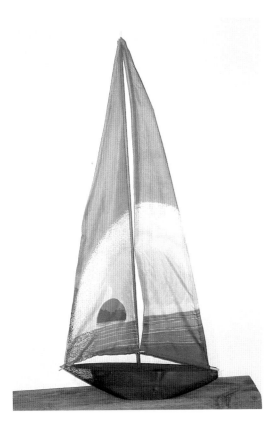

Jenn Williams

Model boat with batik sails
Procion dyes on silk.

Pom Stanley

**Flowing Rhythms
No.1 (5 panels, 100
x 200cm)**
Batik on chiffon
using Dupont dyes.

Bibliography and Further Reading

Noel Dyrenforth, *The Technique of Batik*
(B T Batsford Ltd., London)

Pepin van Roojen, *Batik Design*
(The Pepin Press)

Miep Spee, *Traditional and Modern Batik*
(Kangaroo Press)

Kate Wells, *Fabric Dyeing and Printing*
(Conran Octopus Ltd.)

Nude bathing.

Suppliers

Phone these companies for their mail order catalogues and shop opening hours:

N.E.S. Arnold (general equipment, school suppliers)
Ludlow Hill Road
West Bridgford
Nottingham NG2 6HD
Tel: 0115 – 945 2000

Art Van Go (brushes, dyes, etc.)
16 Hollybush Lane
Datchworth
Knebworth
Herts SG3 6RE
Tel: 01438 – 814946

Candle Makers Supplies (cantings, chemicals, dyes, wax, wax pots)
28 Blythe Road
London W14 0HA
Tel: 0171 – 602 4031

Craft Creations (greetings card blanks and accessories, newsprint)
Ingersoll House
Delamare Road
Cheshunt
Herts EN8 9ND
Tel: 01992 – 781900

Noel Dyrenforth (cantings, Procion dyes)
11 Shepherds Hill
London N6 5QJ
Tel: 0181 – 348 0956

Kemtex Services Ltd. (dyes)
Tameside Business Centre
Wondmill Road
Denton
Manchester M34 3QS
Tel: 0161 – 320 6505

M & R Dyes (dyes and courses in dyeing)
Carters
Station Road
Wickham Bishops
Witham
Essex CM8 3JB
Tel: 01621 – 891405

McCulloch & Wallis (fabrics)
25–26 Dering Street
London W1A 3AX
Tel: 0171 – 409 0725

Pongees (silk)
28–30 Hoxton Square
London N1 6NN
Tel: 0171 – 739 9130

Rainbow Silks (dyes, fabric, equipment)
27 New Road
Amersham
Bucks HP6 6LD
Tel: 01494 – 727003

Suasion (cantings, chemicals, dyes, fabrics, wax pots)
35 Riding House Street
London W1P 7PT
0171 – 580 3763

Landscape *in situ*.

Textile Techniques (cantings, caps,
traditional batik fabrics, wax)
37 High Street
Bishops Castle
Shropshire SY9 5BE
Tel: 01588 – 638712

George Weil & Sons (fabrics)
The Warehouse
Reading Arch Road
Redhill
Surrey RH1 1HG
Tel: 01737 – 778868

Whaleys (Bradford) Ltd. (fabrics)
Harris Court
Great Horton
Bradford
West Yorkshire BD7 4EQ
Tel: 01274 – 56718

Wolfin Textiles (fabrics)
64 Great Titchfield Street
London W1 7AE
Tel: 0171 – 636 4949

Ukrainian Booksellers (kystkas)
49 Linden Gardens
London W2 4HG
Tel: 0171 – 229 0140

For information on The Batik Guild
contact the Membership Secretary on
0171 – 226 3744.

Index

Opposite: Poppy picture
with coloured fabrics in
the foreground.